María José Ferrada is the author of *Mexique: A Refugee Story from the Spanish Civil War* (Eerdmans). She is a recipient of the Municipal Prize of Literature of Santiago, as well as the Academy Award from the Chilean Academy of Language. María currently works as the children's editor of Chilean Memory, a digital resource center of the National Library of Chile.

María Elena Valdez studied art in Caracas, Venezuela. She has illustrated books published across Latin America, and she has also collaborated with World Vision Costa Rica and the International Union for the Conservation of Nature. This is her first book published in English. María lives in Barcelona, Spain. Follow her on Instagram @mariaelena.valdez.a or visit her website at mariaelenavaldez.com.

For Pedro Novakovich.
For Pablo Athanasiu.
And in memory of the children killed and
disappeared during the Chilean dictatorship.

First published in the United States in 2021
by Eerdmans Books for Young Readers,
an imprint of Wm. B. Eerdmans Publishing Co.
Grand Rapids, Michigan

www.eerdmans.com/youngreaders

First published by © Alboroto ediciones, Mexico, 2019
Original title: *Niños*

English language translation copyright © Lawrence
Schimel, 2021

Published in agreement with Phileas Fogg Agency
www.phileasfoggagency.com

Manufactured in China

29 28 27 26 25 24 23 22 21   1 2 3 4 5 6 7 8 9

ISBN 978-0-8028-5567-1

A catalog record of this book is available
from the Library of Congress

Illustrations created with watercolor, graphite, pastel,
charcoal, and colored pencils

MIX
Paper from
responsible sources
FSC
www.fsc.org   FSC® C104723

niños

POEMS FOR THE LOST CHILDREN OF CHILE

María José Ferrada • María Elena Valdez

translated by Lawrence Schimel

EERDMANS BOOKS FOR YOUNG READERS

GRAND RAPIDS, MICHIGAN

Niños

At noon on September 11, 1973, military planes bombed the Palacio de La Moneda in Santiago, the presidential palace of Chile. This violent coup d'état ended the government of President Salvador Allende and began seventeen years of a dictatorship. General Pinochet's regime would not only put an end to democracy in Chile—it would also put an end to the lives of many Chileans. These were seventeen years of silence, seventeen years of pain, seventeen years of mothers, fathers, and children wondering how something like this could happen.

Only in 1990, when democracy returned to Chile, did the world learn the scope of the violence committed against anyone who was declared different. According to reports prepared by the Chilean State from the Rettig Commission and the National Corporation for Reparations and Reconciliation, the number of dead were 3,197 (2,095 had been executed and at least 1,102 had disappeared). Among these numbers were thirty-four children under the age of fourteen.

Thirty-four children: was that possible? Could something like that have happened? We'd like to think that it couldn't, that we were wrong. And yet there were the reports to tell us that humanity—in the saddest and darkest moments of its history— was able to forget its nature and become a monster that devastated everything in its path, even the most fragile and delicate things in the world: children.

This book is an homage to those thirty-four Chilean children, who in these pages play, dream, and listen to the voices of their mothers. Because this is what we think children should do. But this book is also a reminder, an alarm. For we tell this story knowing that at this moment, many children feel afraid, suffer tragedies, and even lose their lives because of political violence. To those children, and to the memory that helps us defeat monsters, we dedicate this book.

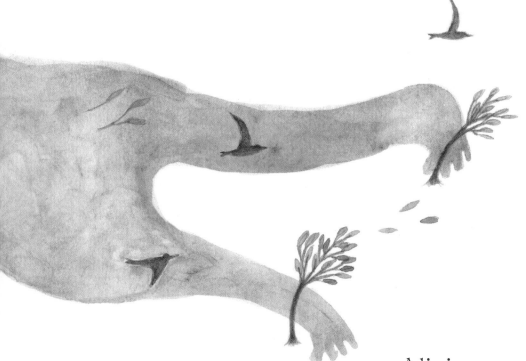

Alicia

Of all the gifts she's been given this birthday
her favorite are the balloons
that decorated the house for the party.
Because if they fly—
if she opens the window and lets them fly—
it would be like giving a gift to the wind.
Because the wind must also have a birthday.
Even if we don't know it, it must have one.

Jaime

He made friends with the bird who lived in the tree outside his window.
He understands its every peep and thinks that if he were small
he could visit its nest in the afternoons.
He could even learn to sing,
and they could make a concert together.

Carmen

There's an apple tree in the yard of her house.
She looks at it and writes in a notebook:
Autumn—leaves.
Winter—branches.
Spring—leaves and shoots.
Summer—fruits.
And at the end, she adds in parentheses:
(The apple tree is a clock
that grows upon the earth.
Instead of telling the hour, it tells the season. Today it's autumn.)

Rafael

Today he decided to search for seven similarities
between the sun and an orange.
It took him an hour to discover them.
And then he left with the orange shining
in his pocket.

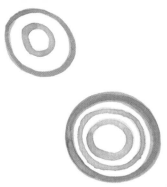

Soledad

She likes the sound that raindrops make
when they fall on the roof of the house.
She knows that each plink is different from the next.
That's why, every time the first rain of the year comes,
on a fogged-up window she writes
a symphony.

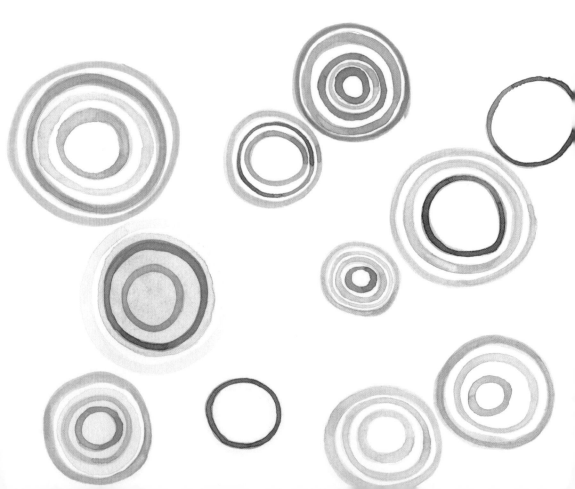

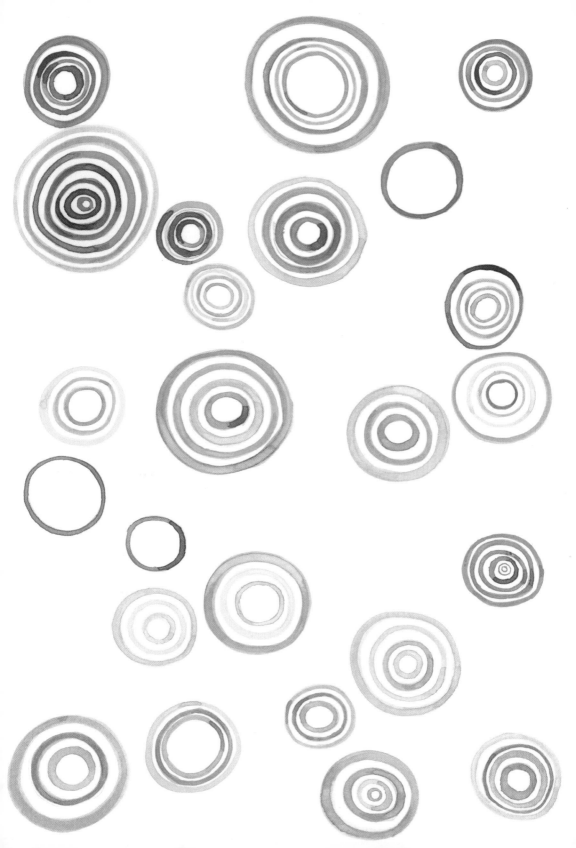

Hugo

He will be a poet.
And he'll create a poem that rhymes
with the *clap-clap* of the soles of his sneakers
in the puddles.

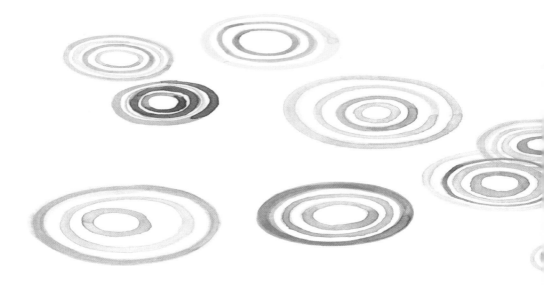

Paola

She saw an insect for the first time.
She was so happy that for the entire morning
her heart didn't stop buzzing.

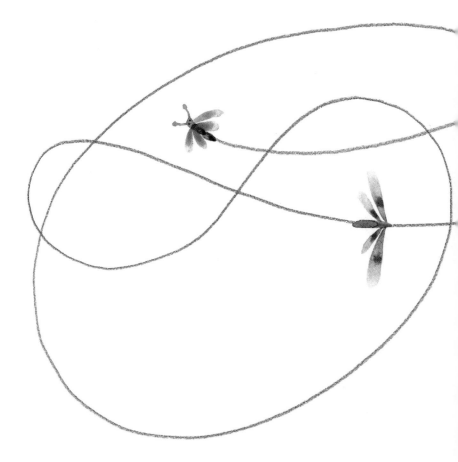

Marcela

She threw a stick,
and her dog brought it back.
When they tired of playing,
the pair lay in the grass to watch how the sun
hid itself at the edge of the city.
Only their hunger reminded them it was time to go home.
It was a perfect afternoon, sweet like licorice.

Luz

When she grows up, she'll be a collector of sounds:
The leaves and the wind.
Her father's footsteps going up the stairs.
The birth of sprouts in the flowerpots.
The song her grandmother sings
to lull her to sleep.
She'll keep them in a matchbox.
That way she can always have them in her pocket,
and take them out whenever she wants to hear them.

Eduardo

He's sure that the best thing about autumn
is watching how the first leaf
decides to separate from the branch—
from the window, watching that flight,
small and yellow.

Samuel

How will he explain that he crossed the entire city
without permission?
That he was following the sun's path,
from the moment it appeared at one point of the city
until it hid itself away in the other.
That he wanted to prove for himself
the fact that Earth is round.

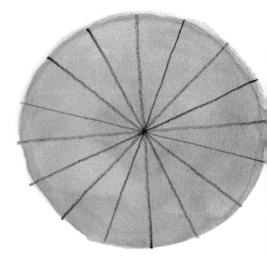

Jessica

She devoted that day to watching the ants.
Each one carried a crumb on its back
and walked along before disappearing over the table's edge.
When nobody was watching, she crumbled a piece of bread
and left it on the floor next to a small letter.
Only with a magnifying glass could you read:
"A gift, for next winter."

Macarena

Three birthday wishes:
to make it summer all year long,
to find the star that sleeps in the middle of apples,
and to discover a secret anthill.

Alejandra

For the first time, she'll see it arrive.
Her mother puts her to sleep
with a song which says that the flowers will come.
A lullaby which says that the birds will come and the sun
will be a small coat.
For the first time: spring.

Magla

If she had to choose a single sound,
she says she'd stick with with the one bubbles make
when they disappear.
With a bit of effort, you can hear it.
She closely watches the small, transparent universes
that begin with this breath and move through the small galaxy
of her house,
then disappear.
Like this: *pop pop pop pop*.

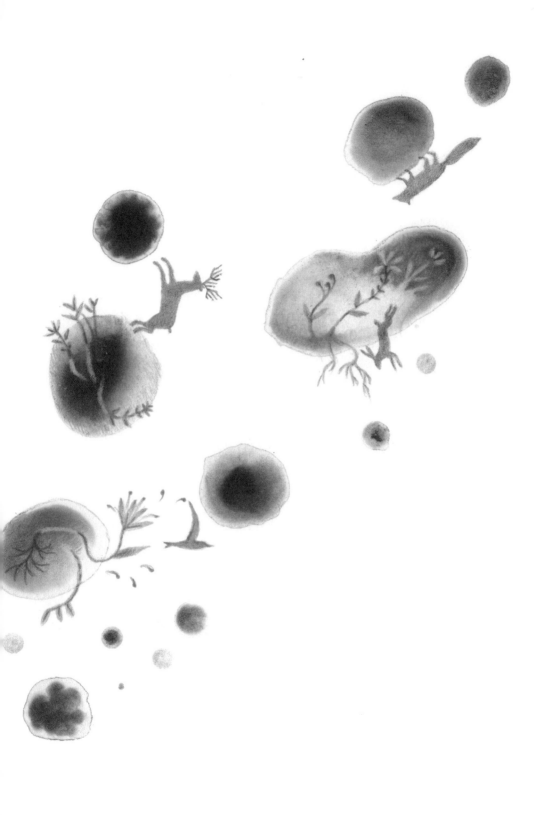

Francisco

After reading *Treasure Island* for the second time he's sure:
pirates are born to find an island
with a shining heart.

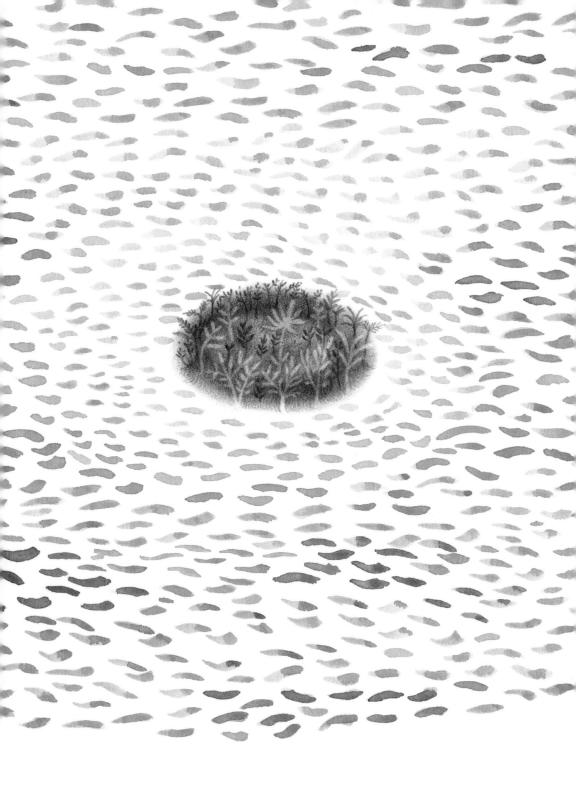

Nadia

With the afternoon rain, a small river formed,
running along the shore of the sidewalk.
She placed three paper boats in the water.
She watched them float away toward the edge of the city.
If it kept raining like this,
she figured that in two days
they would reach the sea.

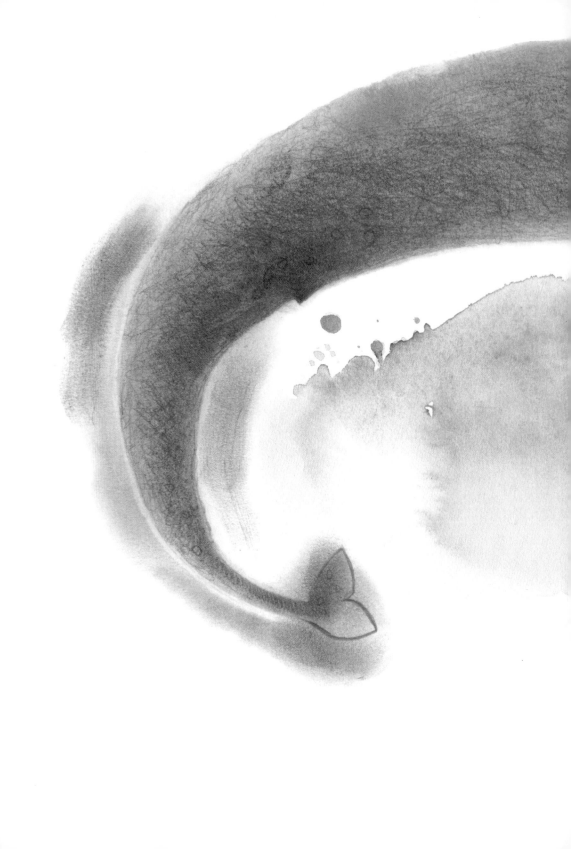

Héctor

He wonders how it's possible for the sound
of the sea
to live inside shells.
He wonders all afternoon.
When night comes, he gives up
and writes it down in his list of mysteries.

Carlos

Every time he sees the light of the lamp,
he wonders if its light speaks in the same language
as the two-million-year-old stars.
If his lamp—instead of a lamp—might be an ancient sigh.

And he falls asleep like that, without turning it off.

Gabriel

He likes to imagine that the stars are holes in the sky.
When the sun hides itself,
the Earth is covered by a black coat.
It is so old it has holes—
thus, those lights.

Susana

Every night she likes to watch how the lights she sees
from her window go out.
Because it's like watching sunsets,
lightning bugs,
tiny lighthouses.

Felipe

He likes to watch
how the lightbulb that illuminates his room
is turned on and off.
It's like a miniature sun.

He wonders if anyone else might have noticed.

Mercedes

That day she made a discovery: the moon
was an enormous cheese.
Sooner or later, the mouse who lived in the patio would realize this.
Then she'd only need to follow it to reach the heavens
and see Earth from up on high.
And if the mouse let her, she would also give the moon
a big bite.

Nelson

He discovered that the moon fits in a glass of water.
That if he puts a glass on the floor at night, just below
the moon,
another is born—so tiny—there inside the water.
The same happens with the stars.
Before going to sleep, he tells his sister the secret:
there's a sky inside the cups.

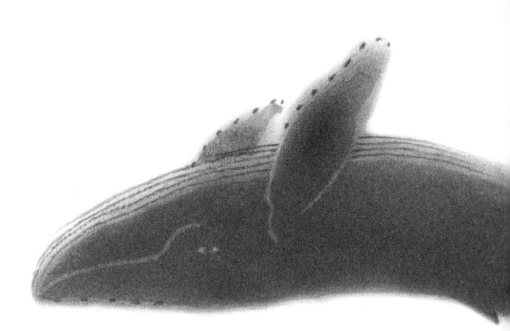

Marco

Rain had begun to fall
and he thought that if he collected all the raindrops
in the buckets in the yard,
he could make something with them.
An ocean, for example.

Claudia

She has spent an hour watching the clouds pass by
and has seen two elephants,
three birds,
and a salamander.
She wonders if anyone else is watching them
from some window.
If another girl like her
saw the parade of white animals.

Lorena

She has an imaginary friend with no shoes;
that's why nobody hears him
when he comes up the stairs.
But she does.
She can hear *tic-tic tic-tic tic-tic*.
And she can speak to him in his language for hours on end.

Elizabeth

Today she would be the teacher
and ask questions to her students:
a stuffed bear and a doll.

Where did yellow come from?
    a. It came from the edge of the honeypot.
    b. It came from the field of sunflowers.
    c. It appeared in the sky in the shape of a circle.
    d. All of the above.

José

He decided to invent his own dictionary.
To group words together in a new way.
Words wrapped in coats: *honey, Mama, sun, sparrow.*
Fantastic words: *rainbow, night, planet.*
Luminous words: *star, grandfather, grasshopper.*
And so on.

Orlando

He spent the afternoon drawing insects.
He took them to the garden and had them march in single file.
From the smallest to the biggest.
Little by little they lost their order: some went through the grass
and others climbed the branches of the apple tree.
Finally, he lost sight of them. That's what happens with bugs.

330

284

338

Jaime

He will count all the flowers of the world
that fit in a single spring.
Then he will classify them by scent and color.
He will begin with those growing on his street.

Raúl

His mother called him "little bird."
And he likes the way that sounds.
Little bird.

Sergio

That spring he decided
he would plant words in a flowerpot.
He would carefully water the seeds.
The seasons would pass.
He would watch them bloom.

This list of the thirty-three children arrested, disappeared, and executed was created with information gathered by the National Commission for Truth and Reconciliation (Rettig Commission) and by the National Corporation for Reparations and Reconciliation. Thirty-two were executed, and one remains listed as arrested and disappeared.

The author of this book would like to thank Victoria Baeza, tireless worker for human rights, for her collaboration in the difficult process of reviewing reports.

Alicia Marcela Aguilar Carvajal
killed; 6 years old

Jaime Andrés Cáceres Morales
killed; 11 years old

Carmen Ximena Pizarro Nova
killed; 10 years old

Rafael Antonio Gallardo Arancibia
killed; 6 years old

Soledad Ester Torres Aguayo
killed; 4 years old

Hugo Abraham Rodríguez Mena
killed; 8 years old

Paola Andrea Torres Aguayo
killed; 3 years old

Marcela Angélica Marchant Vivar
killed; 8 years old

Luz Marina Paineman Puel
killed; 1 month old

Eduardo Elías Cerda Ángel
killed; 8 years old

Samuel Roberto Castro Castro
killed; 13 years old

Jessica del Carmen Riffo Troncoso
killed; 9 years old

Macarena Denisse Torres Tello
killed; 6 years old

Alejandra del Carmen Berríos Valencia
killed; 1 month old

Magla Evelyn Ayala Henríquez
killed; 2 years old

Francisco Antonio Fuenzalida Morales
killed; 12 years old

Nadia del Carmen Fuentes Concha
killed; 13 years old

Héctor Enrique González Yáñez
killed; 8 years old

Carlos Patricio Fariña Oyarce
killed; 13 years old

Gabriel Enrique Flores Poblete
killed; 3 years old

Susana Elizabeth Sanhueza Salinas
killed; 3 years old

Felipe Antonio Gutiérrez Garrido
killed; 2 years old

Mercedes del Pilar Corredero Reyes
killed; 9 years old

Nelson Luis Hormazábal Pino
killed; 2 years old

Marco Antonio Navarrete Clavijo
killed; 10 years old

Claudia Andrea Valenzuela Velásquez
killed; 6 years old

Lorena del Pilar Escobar Lagos
killed; 3 years old

Elizabeth del Carmen Venegas
Muñoz killed; 13 years old

José Orlando Jara Latorre
killed; 13 years old

Orlando José Sáez Pérez
killed; 9 years old

Jaime Ignacio Rojas Rojas
killed; 9 years old

Raúl Armando Sepúlveda Catrileo
killed; 5 months old

Sergio Arturo Gómez Arriagada
disappeared; 11 years old

Pablo

When I grow up I'll be a tree, a cloud,
a wave,
a snail.
And all those shapes
that can be seen in the clouds I've learned to stare at.
A tree, a cloud, a wave, a snail.
When I learn to speak,
these words will be the first things I'll say.

Pablo Athanasiu, victim of a system of persecution and extermination that knew no borders, was part of this list until August 7, 2013, the day when the Abuelas of the Plaza de Mayo found him alive. We dedicate this book to him and hope the stars always shine for him.